10 Experiments Your Teacher Never Told You About

Andrew Solway

Raintree

www.raintreepublishers.co.uk

Visit our website to find out more information about **Raintree** books.

To order:
☎ Phone 44 (0) 1865 888112
🗎 Send a fax to 44 (0) 1865 314091
💻 Visit the Raintree bookshop at **www.raintreepublishers.co.uk** to browse our catalogue and order online.

First published in Great Britain by Raintree, Halley Court, Jordan Hill, Oxford OX2 8EJ, part of Harcourt Education.
Raintree is a registered trademark of Harcourt Education Ltd.

Editorial: Lucy Thunder and Richard Woodham
Design: Michelle Lisseter, Carolyn Gibson, and Bigtop
Illustrations: Darren Lingard
Picture Research: Melissa Allison and Fiona Orbell
Production: Camilla Crask

Originated by Dot Gradations Ltd
Printed and bound in Italy by Printer Trento srl

ISBN 1 844 43847 3
10 09 08 07 06
10 9 8 7 6 5 4 3 2 1

British Library Cataloguing in Publication Data
Solway, Andrew
10 Experiments Your Teacher Never Told You About: Gravity
531.1′4
A full catalogue record for this book is available from the British Library.

Acknowledgements
The publishers would like to thank the following for permission to reproduce photographs:
Airsport p. 12–13; Corbis pp. 4–5 (NASA/Roger Ressmeyer); Getty Images p. 26–27 (Photodisc); NASA p. 16–17; Science Photo Library pp. 8–9 (NASA), 10–11 (Erich Schrempp), 20–21 (Roger Harris).

Cover photograph of the Earth from space reproduced with permission of Science Photo Library.

The publishers would like to thank Nancy Harris and Harold Pratt for their assistance in the preparation of this book.

Every effort has been made to contact copyright holders of any material reproduced in this book. Any omissions will be rectified in subsequent printings if notice is given to the publishers.

The paper used to print this book comes from sustainable resources.

Disclaimer
All the Internet addresses (URLs) given in this book were valid at the time of going to press. However, due to the dynamic nature of the Internet, some addresses may have changed, or sites may have changed or ceased to exist since publication. While the author and publishers regret any inconvenience this may cause readers, no responsibility for any such changes can be accepted by either the author or the publishers.

Contents

Some words are printed in bold, **like this**. You can find out what they mean on page 30. You can also look in the box at the bottom of the page where they first appear.

Holding everything together

What do you do in science lessons at school? Do you go skydiving? Do you take a rocket to the Moon? No? Well, here is your chance! This book is about **gravity** experiments. They are experiments that you could never do at school.

Gravity is a **force**. A force is a push or pull. Gravity pulls on Earth, the Moon, and the stars in space. Earth, the Moon, and stars are parts of the **universe**. Gravity holds the universe together. Look around you. Just about everything is held on to Earth by gravity. Without gravity, cars, animals, people, and everything else would float off into space.

force	a push or pull
gravity	force that pulls objects together
universe	everything that exists anywhere

◀ *Have you ever wondered what it's like to fly into space?*

Experiment 1: Proving the basics

You will need a bag of apples for this experiment. Take an apple out of the bag and drop it. It falls to the ground because of **gravity**. On Earth, gravity is the **force** that pulls everything towards the ground. Now throw an apple upwards. It does not keep going up. Gravity pulls it back towards the ground.

Have you tried dropping an apple below Earth's surface, in a deep hole? If you do, you will find that gravity pulls the apple down below the ground. This is because gravity doesn't stop at Earth's surface. It pulls everything towards the centre of Earth.

▲ Wherever you drop
an apple, it will
fall downwards.

Experiment 2: Gravity on the Moon

Would you like to take a trip to the Moon? We are going there to find out how **gravity** and **mass** are connected.

Mass is how much there is of an object. For example, an elephant has more mass than a mouse.

All objects have a pull of gravity. All objects pull on each other. The pull of gravity from an object depends on its mass. A huge object such as Earth has a huge mass. Earth's pull of gravity is strong. You have a very small mass compared to Earth. Your force of gravity is very, very weak.

mass   how much there is of an object

Let's take that trip to the Moon. As soon as you get out of the rocket, you will feel the difference. Try to jump. You won't have any trouble breaking the world high jump record!

You feel light. This is because the Moon has much less mass than Earth. This means the pull of gravity on the Moon is also less.

▲ *Astronauts can bounce around on the surface of the Moon. This is because the pull of gravity is less on the Moon than on the Earth.*

Experiment 3: Two watermelons

In this experiment we will look closely at falling. When you drop something, **gravity** pulls it towards the ground. It falls faster and faster. It **accelerates.** One way to prove this is to take a set of photos very quickly of something falling. The photo on the right shows a ball falling.

As this ball fell, ▶ *a photo was taken every one-tenth of a second. As it accelerated, the ball moved further between each photo.*

accelerate   to go faster

Our experiment is much easier. Take two juicy watermelons to the park. Drop one from a height of 30 centimetres (12 inches). Thump! The watermelon hits the ground. It does not smash open. Next, get in a helicopter and fly up until the park looks the size of a tissue. Now drop your second melon. The second melon falls further. Gravity accelerates the melon. It makes the melon hit the ground at a faster speed.

▲ *SPLAT! There are bits of watermelon everywhere!*

Experiment 4: Free fall!

In this experiment you'll be doing some more falling. You are going to jump out of an aeroplane. You will free fall for 30 seconds.

Ready to jump? Go! You are falling faster and faster. You are **accelerating**. Wow, the wind is so noisy!

Now what's happening? You are still falling very fast. But you aren't accelerating any more. You're not getting any faster. Why not?

The clue is the wind. Falling through the air this fast is like walking into a very strong wind. A **force** pushes on your body. This force is called **air resistance**. It pushes your body in the opposite direction from the force of **gravity**.

*Strong winds push ▶
against your face
as you fall.*

air resistance   force that slows down an object moving through air
constant   staying the same

Gravity pulls you down. But air resistance pushes back. The two forces are in balance. This means you stop accelerating. You fall at a **constant** speed. Your speed does not change.

Experiment 5: In a hole

How can we show that **gravity** pulls things to the centre of Earth?

First we need a hole through the centre of Earth. It will have to be imaginary. It's too hard to dig.

It's time to jump into the hole. At first, gravity pulls you down. You fall faster and faster. Soon, you fall right through the centre of Earth. Now gravity starts pulling you back towards the centre of Earth.

You slow down, then start falling the other way. You fall back through the centre of Earth, where the pull of gravity changes again. It's like a bungee jump, but without the rope!

Air resistance slows you down in the end. You stop at Earth's centre. Gravity really does pull everything towards the centre of Earth.

At first, gravity pulls you down.

centre of Earth

centre of Earth

Gravity starts pulling you back towards the centre of Earth.

centre of Earth

In the end you stop at Earth's centre.

Experiment 6: Back to the Moon

Where can we find out how the pull of **gravity** and **mass** are connected to weight? We'll need to go back to the Moon.

Your mass is how much there is of you. Wherever you are in the **universe**, your mass stays the same. This is because there is always the same amount of you. But when you were on the Moon in Experiment 2, you felt lighter. Does this mean your weight can change?

First, you need to weigh yourself on Earth. Let's say you weigh 42 kilograms (92 pounds). Then take a quick trip to the Moon. Get on those weighing scales again. Now you only weigh 7 kilograms (15 pounds)!

Your weight depends on the **force** of gravity. The smaller the force of gravity, the less your weight. The force of gravity on Earth is six times the force of gravity on the Moon. So on the Moon you weigh about one-sixth of your weight on Earth.

A lasting impression

There is no air on the Moon. Winds do not blow like they do on Earth. This means that astronaut footprints will stay there for millions of years!

▲ An astronaut weighs less on the Moon even with a big spacesuit on.

Experiment 7: A ladder into space

On Earth the **force** of **gravity** pulls things towards the centre of Earth. But does gravity change as you move further away from the centre of Earth? You will find out in this experiment.

You will need a weight, a spring balance, and a very tall ladder. Climb the ladder until you are 6,378 kilometres (3,963 miles) above Earth. You are now twice as far from the centre of the Earth as you were at the surface. This means you are twice as far from the centre of Earth's force of gravity.

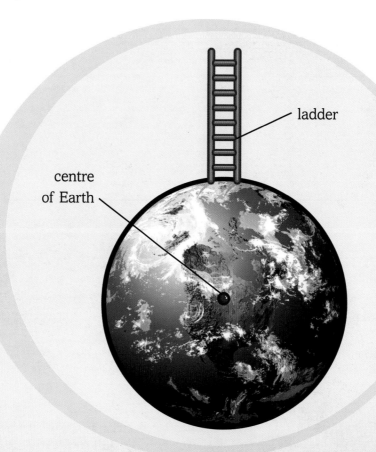

ladder

centre
of Earth

At this height, you might think the force of gravity will be half as strong. On Earth the weight was 1 kilogram (2 pounds). The weight should weigh half as much up here as it did on Earth.

But it only weighs 0.25 kilograms (0.5 pounds)! The force of gravity is only a quarter as strong. Gravity gets weaker as things move further away from each other. This happens faster than you might expect.

weight

▲ Gravity gets weaker the further away from Earth you are.

Experiment 8: Into orbit

In Experiment 7 we showed there was **gravity** 6,378 kilometres (3,963 miles) above Earth. But the Space Shuttle is circling around Earth only 300 kilometres (186 miles) above the surface.

So why doesn't the **force** of gravity pull it down? In fact, gravity does pull it down. But gravity also keeps it in **orbit**. Gravity keeps it circling around Earth.

To find out how, you will need your very, very tall ladder again. Climb it until you are 300 kilometres (186 miles) high. From here, you will use a robot arm to throw a ball.

▼ The force of gravity keeps a Space Shuttle from crashing down to Earth.

Throw one

Let's start with a throw of about 160 kilometres (100 miles) per hour. It's gone a long way. Now it's falling. It has landed a few kilometres away from the ladder.

Throw two

Try a harder throw of about 1,600 kilometres (1,000 miles) per hour. Wow, the ball seems to be flying! But now it's beginning to dip down. Yes, it's falling. Gravity has pulled it down to the ground at last.

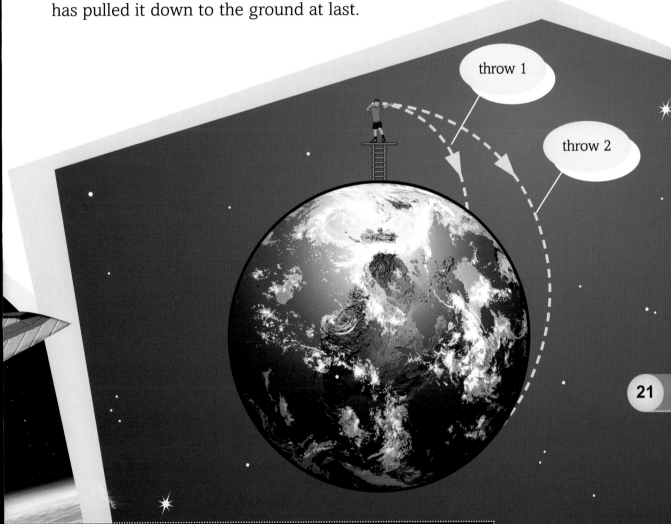

throw 1

throw 2

21

orbit   when one object moves in a path around another object

The last throw

Let's try a throw at full power. Wow! The ball has gone off at 27,800 kilometres (17,300 miles) per hour! It just keeps going. It's flying right around Earth. It's in **orbit**!

Why doesn't the ball fall to the ground? Actually it does fall, but it misses Earth. The forward speed of the ball is trying to take it away from Earth. At the same time **gravity** is trying to pull it down. Gravity stops the ball flying off into space. But gravity does not pull enough to make the ball fall to the ground.

If you throw a ball from the ground, a **force** called **air resistance** pushes back on it. Air resistance makes the ball slow down. But in space there is no air. There is no air resistance. The ball does not slow down.

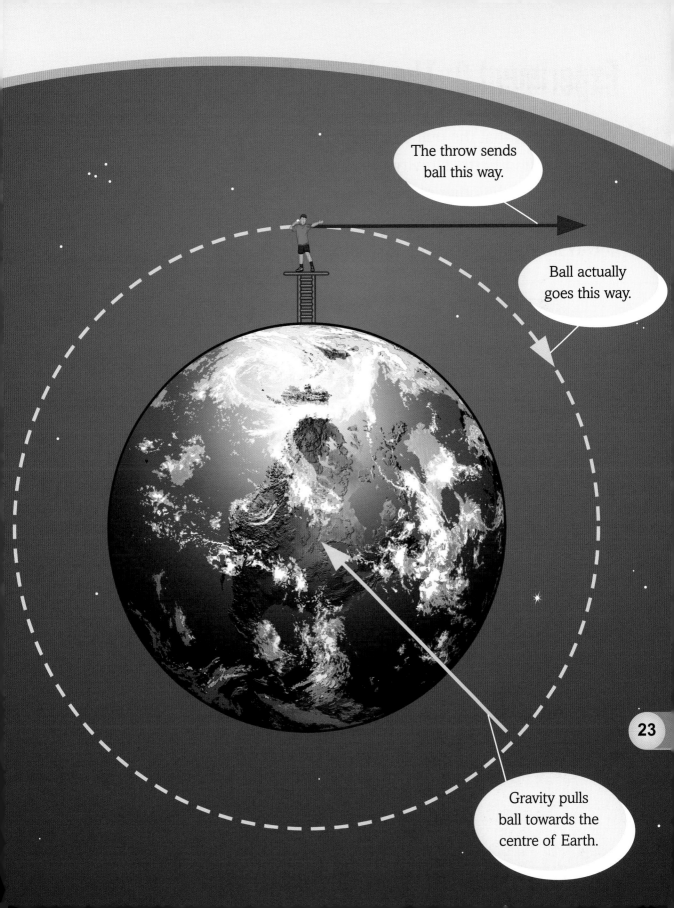

Experiment 9: The disappearing Sun

We have seen that the pull of **gravity** keeps the Moon circling around Earth. Gravity keeps the Moon in **orbit**. But Earth and the other planets also orbit the Sun. The Sun's pull of gravity is very strong. The pull of the Sun's gravity keeps the planets in their orbits.

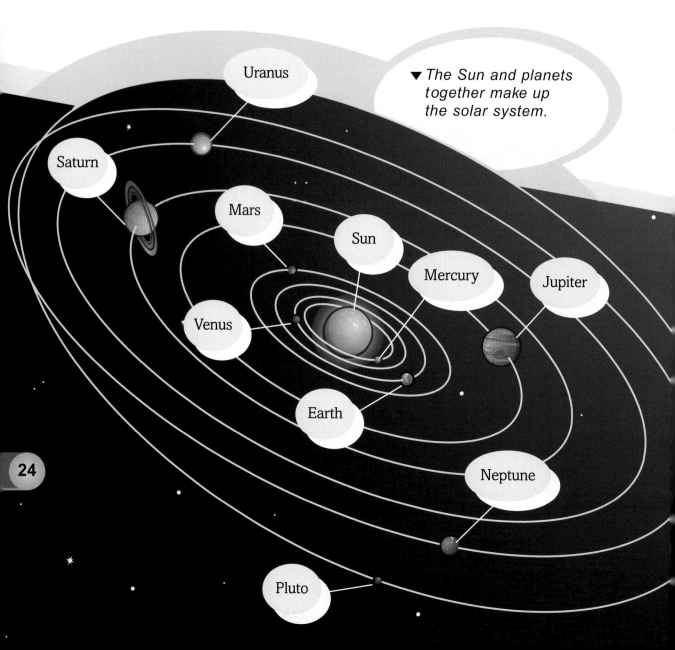

▼ The Sun and planets together make up the solar system.

What would happen if the Sun wasn't there? To find out, we'll imagine we have an invention that can turn off the gravity of the Sun. But it will only be for a minute.

Are you ready? The Sun's gravity is going off now! Oh no! The planets aren't staying in their orbits. They are shooting off in straight lines. Quick turn it back on!

That was a disaster! It will be a huge job to get all the planets back in their orbits.

▼ The arrows show how the planets would shoot off if the Sun's gravity was turned off.

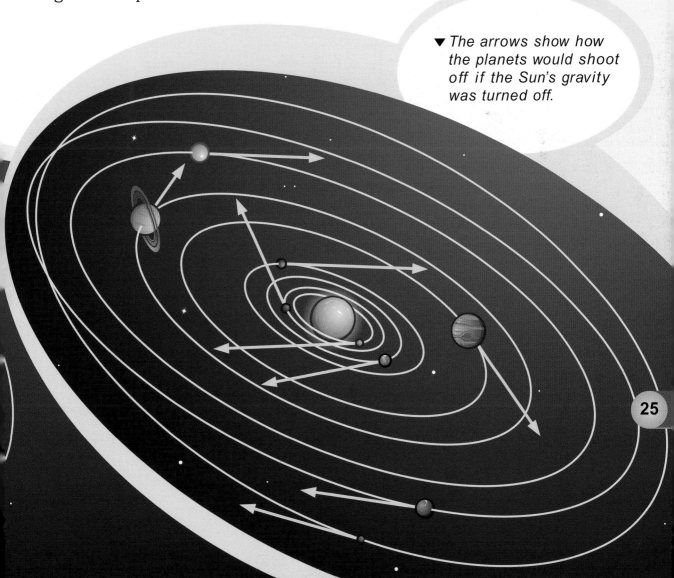

Experiment 10: Your head is the Sun

Let's do a simple experiment to show why the planets shot off in Experiment 9.

Take a tennis ball and attach a piece of string to it. Now take your tennis ball and string outside. Hold the string and swing the ball around your head. The tennis ball circles your head like a planet **orbits** the Sun. The string keeping the ball in orbit is the **force** of **gravity**.

We can easily see what happens without gravity. Just let go of the string. The tennis ball flies off in a straight line.

Well, that's the end of our gravity experiments. Now that you know more about the force of gravity, you will notice it everywhere. Gravity is the glue that holds our **universe** together!

String acts like the force of gravity.

Isaac Newton

*The scientist Isaac Newton showed that if there is no **force** working on a moving object, it stays still or goes in a straight line. The Sun's gravity is the main force working on the planets. Without it, they would move in straight lines.*

The force of gravity ▲ keeps everything together in the universe.

Things to remember about gravity

Any two objects in the ▶ **universe** are pulled towards each other by the **force** of **gravity**.

An object with a large ▼ **mass** has a strong force of gravity.

◀An object with a small mass has a weak force of gravity.

◀Mass is different from weight. An object's mass stays the same. But its weight changes with gravity. The smaller the force of gravity, the less the weight.

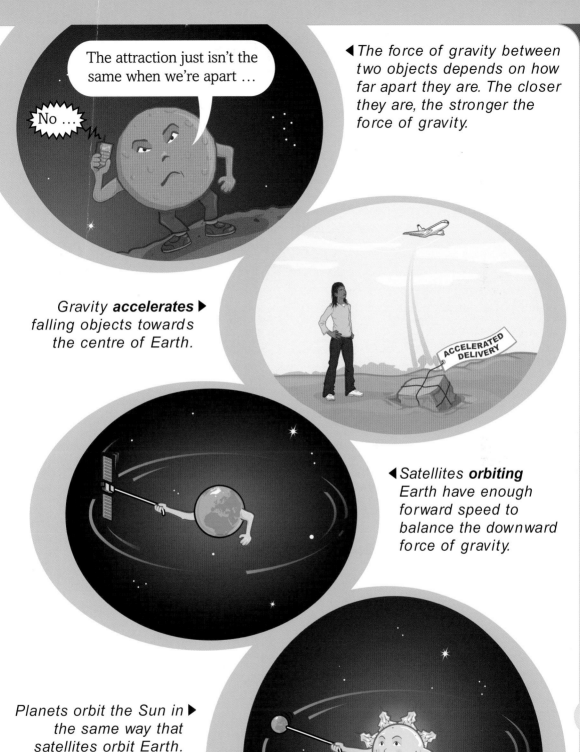

The attraction just isn't the same when we're apart …

No …

◀ The force of gravity between two objects depends on how far apart they are. The closer they are, the stronger the force of gravity.

Gravity **accelerates** ▶ falling objects towards the centre of Earth.

ACCELERATED DELIVERY

◀ Satellites **orbiting** Earth have enough forward speed to balance the downward force of gravity.

Planets orbit the Sun in ▶ the same way that satellites orbit Earth.

Glossary

accelerate to go faster. The force of gravity accelerates objects falling towards the ground.

air resistance force that slows down an object moving through air. Aeroplanes and cars have smooth shapes to cut down their air resistance.

constant staying the same. The speed of a car is constant if it does not change.

force a push or pull. When you roll down a hill on your bike without pedalling, the force of gravity pulls you along.

gravity force that pulls objects together. Planets and the Sun are large enough to have strong gravity.

mass how much there is of an object. The mass of an object stays the same even if the pull of gravity changes.

orbit when one object moves in a path around another object. Earth and the other planets orbit the Sun.

universe everything that exists anywhere. The universe includes Earth, the Sun, and all the other stars and planets in space.

Want to know more?

Books

- *Dead Famous: Isaac Newton and his Apple*, Kjartan Poskitt (Scholastic Hippo, 1999)
- *Gravity*, Don Nardo (Kidhaven, 2003)
- *Routes of Science: Gravity*, Chris Woodford (Blackbirch, 2004)
- *Science World: The Science of Gravity*, John Stringer (Hodder Wayland, 1999)
- *True Books: Science Experiments, Experiments with Gravity*, Salvatore Tocci (Children's Press, 2002)

Websites

- Try to keep five planets orbiting the Sun, or find out how gravity affects your cannon shots in a sea battle at: library.thinkquest.org/27585/frameset_intro.html
- Work out how to get the most thrilling ride on a roller coaster at: www.funderstanding.com/k12/coaster You can even change gravity to increase the thrills!

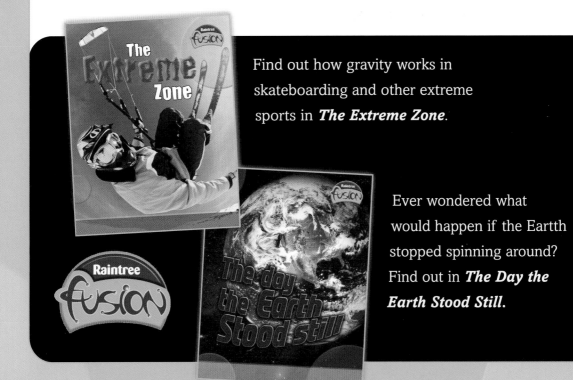

Find out how gravity works in skateboarding and other extreme sports in *The Extreme Zone*.

Ever wondered what would happen if the Eartth stopped spinning around? Find out in *The Day the Earth Stood Still.*

Index